# GLOSSARY NOTES

# The Secret Garden

HERON BOOKS
K-12 CURRICULUM

*Published by*
**Heron Books, Inc.**
20950 SW Rock Creek Road
Sheridan, OR 97378
heronbooks.com

First Edition © 2008, 2018, Heron Books
All Rights Reserved

ISBN # 0-89739-088-1

Printed in the USA

22 November 2018

# Contents

# About this Glossary

This glossary may be used to help you enjoy *The Secret Garden* by Frances Hodgson Burnett. It provides information and definitions for unusual words and phrases not likely found in a dictionary at this level.

The words are defined in the order they appear in the book, and only the first time they appear. An alphabetical word list is provided at the back of the glossary.

# Notes on Yorkshire, England

## YORKSHIRE

Yorkshire is a large area in northeastern England. It is full of fields, hills and winding valleys. In much of Yorkshire, the people have been farmers for hundreds of years.

## YORKSHIRE WAY OF SPEAKING.

The people of this region speak English in a way that we call "Yorkshire English," "Yorkshire speech," or just "Yorkshire." It's a more old-fashioned and easy, flowing way of speaking English and, in the story, some of the characters speak it. Here are some points that will help in reading Yorkshire speech:

- Hundreds of years ago, English people would say *thou* and *thee* instead of *you*. For example, *Thou speakest too loudly* or *I want to give thee this present.* In Yorkshire speech, *thou* was pronounced "tha."

- Instead of *your*, people said *thy*. For example, *I love thy new dress.*

- Old-fashioned forms of verbs are used sometimes, such as *art* for *are*, *wert* for *were*, etc.

- Often *us* is said instead of *we*, for example, *Us used to wonder about it.*

• Yorkshire people sometimes drop off the ends of words. For example, they might say *th'* for *the*, *an'* for *and*, *growin'* for *growing*, *o'* for *of*, *enow* for *enough*, *himsel'* for *himself*, or *kep'* for *kept*.

## READING DIALOGUE (CONVERSATION) ALOUD

When characters in *The Secret Garden* are speaking Yorkshire to each other, the author usually writes it the way it *sounds* to make it more realistic.

Here's a passage from the story, first written in modern English and then as it actually appears in the book in Yorkshire:

> "What have you been doing with yourself—hiding out of sight and letting people think you were crippled and half-witted?"

> "What's tha' been doin' with thysel'—hidin' out o' sight an' lettin' folk think tha' was cripple and half-witted?"

Reading these parts aloud will usually help make them easier to understand.

# Glossary

# Glossary

## Chapter 1

**skin was yellow:** sometimes when a person is ill with certain diseases, especially in places with hot climates like India, their skin turns yellowish.

**English Government:** In the 1800s and early 1900s, India was England's most important colony. Many English men held positions in the English military, government and businesses there and brought their wives and children from England to live with them. Mary's father works for the English Government in India.

**Ayah:** a native Indian woman hired as a nanny.

**Mem Sahib:** the polite, respectful way Indian people spoke to a European woman. (The word *Sahib* by itself meant "friend" and was the polite term used by the Indian people for a European man. "Mem Sahib" came from saying *Ma'am Sahib*.)

**fretful:** irritable and always complaining; worried or annoyed.

**toddling thing:** a very young child who walks unsteadily; toddler.

**familiarly:** in a very personal way, like one's family.

**pig:** *(informal)* a person who is unpleasant and difficult to deal with.

**learn her letters:** learn how to read and write.

**passion:** loud, emotional outburst.

**Missie Sahib:** the polite term Indian people used when talking to a European girl.

**garden:** *(British)* the area surrounding a house or building; yard. A garden is planted with flowers, trees and grass, usually has pathways and is enclosed by walls or hedges.

**Saidie:** the name of Mary's Ayah (see earlier entry).

**imploringly:** asking in a pleading way.

**You ought to have gone to the hills two weeks ago:** The British also had settlements in the foothills of the Himalayas, northern India. British doctors believed the cooler climate of the mountains was healthier and sent the women and children there during the hottest months of the year and whenever disease broke out in the hotter lowlands.

**servants' quarters:** the places on an estate where the servants live. In this story, they lived in separate little houses on the same property as Mary's larger house.

**it had broken out:** the illness had begun suddenly.

**fatal form:** the type that most people die from.

**dying like flies:** dying quickly in great numbers.

**strong:** describing a drink that contains a lot of alcohol.

**compound:** a group of houses owned by one family. In this case, Mary's compound includes her house and the little houses of servants.

**Mercy on us:** an exclamation of surprise, short for "God have mercy on us."

## Chapter 2

**Mistress Mary Quite Contrary:** a well-known English nursery rhyme.

**self-absorbed:** thinking only about oneself and one's own interests.

**impudent blue eyes:** eyes (blue, in this case) with a look that shows the person is overly bold and has little respect for others.

**rockery:** a garden where plants are arranged to grow around rocks in a decorative way.

**mantle with jet fringe:** a "mantle" is a loose, sleeveless article of clothing that goes over other clothes, sometimes with a hood, sometimes connecting at the throat. "Jet" is a black stone that polishes to a bright shine. "Fringe" is a border of threads, in this case strung with jet beads.

**plain little piece of goods:** "Plain" means not good-looking. "Goods" actually means things that are for sale. Of course, Mary is not for sale but Mrs. Medlock is evaluating her in the same way she would evaluate something she wanted to buy.

**common, highly colored face:** low class, reddish face. "Common" here means a lower class, working person. Mary and her family are members of a higher class who would employ servants. "Highly colored" refers to the tan or reddish color a face gets from being outside and working.

**common fine bonnet:** low quality bonnet even though it was Mrs. Medlock's fine (dress-up) one.

**Yorkshire:** a large region in northeastern England. See the beginning of the glossary for more information.

**railway carriage:** an older name for a passenger car on a train.

**"stand no nonsense from young ones":** not allow any misbehavior from children.

**trunk:** a strong box with a hinged lid used to carry clothes and other belongings while traveling.

**black crepe hat:** "Crepe" is a thin, crinkled, lightweight material. Until recent times, black crepe hats or veils, along with a black dress, were worn by Christian women or girls as a form of respect for someone who had recently died.

**pettish:** easily irritated or annoyed.

**unresponsive:** not showing that she understood or was going to answer.

**Not but that:** *(British)* even though; although something is true, something else is also true.

**park:** *(British)* an area of land around a large house in the countryside. It is usually woodland or other natural land rather than the gardens closer to the house where things are planted and cared for.

**gardens:** There are usually several kinds of gardens grown around a large English country house. For example, there can be formal gardens sometimes with fountains that are carefully planted and clipped to decorate the front of the house. There are usually kitchen gardens in the back, outside the kitchen door, where the herbs, fruits and vegetables for cooking are grown. Gardens will have different purposes and appearances depending on the desires of the owner.

**attracted:** got her interest or attention.

**a trifle:** a little bit.

**Riquet a la Houppe:** the name of the hunchback prince in this French fairy tale.

**West Wing:** A "wing" is a section of a building sticking out from the main part. The "West Wing" of Misselthwaite Manor is built on the west side of the main building.

**Pitcher:** the last name of Mr. Craven's personal servant.

**ten to one:** in ten tries there is only one chance that something will happen; in other words, it's not very likely to happen.

## Chapter 3

**lunchbasket:** a basket packed with food and drink similar to a picnic basket. At this time (early 1900s), baskets of food could be purchased at the train stations. Sometimes, train personnel would take the passengers' orders for food, telegraph them ahead and have the food waiting at the next station for passengers to buy.

**waterproofs:** *(British)* raincoats; coats made from waterproof cloth.

**station-master:** person in charge of a train station.

**rough:** in a simple, plain way, without using special manners or words or being careful how you act or say something.

**pronouncing his words in a queer broad fashion:** saying his words strongly in the Yorkshire way of speaking, which seemed odd to Mary. "Broad" in this sentence describes speech that has a strong accent when heard by someone from a different area.

**tha's:** thou has. Today we would say "you have."

**An' tha's browt th' young 'un with thee:** And thou has (you have) brought the young one with thee (you).

**How's thy Missus?:** How is your Mistress (a word for wife that was used in earlier times)?

**Well enow:** Well enough.

**brougham:** a closed carriage drawn by a single horse with the driver's seat outside.

**footman:** uniformed man servant who waits on the carriage and table of his master and does other jobs also. The name footman originally meant a servant who ran ahead of his master's carriage and did whatever errands or jobs were needed.

**mounted the box:** climbed up on the driver's seat.

**public house:** *(British)* a place where anyone (the public) could buy food and drinks, usually alcoholic drinks. It is commonly called a pub.

**highroad:** *(British)* main road, usually in a town or village.

**gorse:** an evergreen bush with thick green leaves, thorns and fragrant yellow flowers that grows wild in western Europe.

**lodge:** *(British)* a small house on the grounds of a large country house, usually near the main gate and occupied by a gatekeeper, gardener, etc.

**at all events:** anyway; no matter what else happens.

**park gates:** gates that mark the entrance to the park (defined in Chapter 2) around Misselthwaite Manor.

**avenue:** driveway often lined with trees.

**lowbuilt:** possibly having some rooms with a lower roof than the rest of the house.

**ramble:** spread out randomly.

**stone court:** a cobblestoned area mostly surrounded by buildings (the manor house, stables, etc.).

**hall:** *(British)* the central room in a house leading from the front door to other rooms. It was the main gathering place, usually with a grand fireplace.

**flight of steps:** a stairway between one floor and the next.

## Chapter 4

**hearth-rug:** a small rug on the floor in front of the fireplace.

**th':** the.

**tha:** thou. Today we would say "you."

**tha'rt:** thou are. Today we would say "you are."

**an':** and.

**It's none bare:** It's not bare at all.

**It's covered wi' growin' things as smells sweet:** It's covered with growing things that smell sweet.

**It's fair lovely in spring an' summer when th' gorse an' broom an' heather's in flower:** It's fairly (completely; really) lovely in spring and summer when the gorse (bush with thick green leaves, thorns and yellow flowers) and broom (bush with small green leaves on slender branches and yellow flowers) and heather (low bush with tiny purple flowers) is in flower.

**o':** of.

**salaams:** low bows, made with the right hand touching the forehead.

**blackingbrush:** a brush used to spread a black paste on the metal frame that held the coal for Mary's fire. When the black paste dried, the metal frame was polished to a shine.

**without seeming the least out of temper:** without seeming to be at all angry or annoyed.

**under housemaids:** servants who clean, tend fires, carry water and do other work under a senior housemaid or housekeeper. Martha works under Mrs. Medlock. Normally in a grand house only the housekeeper and upstairs maids have contact with the master and family of the house.

**scullery-maid:** the lowest of maids who washes dishes and does the dirtiest jobs in the kitchen.

**let upstairs:** work upstairs as a lady's maid who has contact with the family members.

**gave me the place**: gave me the position (of housemaid).

**Canna' tha' dress thysen!**: Cannot thou (you) dress thyself (yourself)!

**blacks**: In England at this time, the term "black" was used to refer to all colored people, not only those from Africa. Most people from India have dark skin.

**a black's a man an' a brother**: a black person was recognized as a human being. "Am I not a man and a brother?" was an anti-slavery motto that meant "Am I not a human being also, even though my skin is dark?"

**button boots**: shoe-like boots that went up over the ankle and were fastened with buttons instead of laces.

**sixteen shilling**: There were 20 shillings to a British pound. Sixteen shillings at that time would be worth about $96.00 today. (Martha says "sixteen shilling" instead of "sixteen shillings" because it was common to say plural amounts of money in the singular form, for example, "He works for ten pound a month," or "She paid four shilling for the dress.")

**my mother's put to it**: my mother has great difficulty.

**Our Dickon**: Dickon is the name of Martha's brother. Part of the Yorkshire way of speaking is to refer to family members with "our." So instead of Martha saying "my brother, Dickon" she says "our Dickon."

**scarce**: scarcely or almost never; rarely.

**plain enough**: easily enough.

**day out:** day off from work.

**tha'lt:** thou will just. Today we would say "you will just."

**tha'll:** thou will. Today we would say "you will."

**clipped borders:** Borders are strips of flowerbeds along the edges of paths or walls in a garden. They are usually planted with flowers that live for several years, so in winter they must be clipped (cut back) to stay neatly along the edge of the path or wall they decorate.

**playing:** flowing.

**kitchen-gardens:** gardens in the back of the house outside the kitchen where the fruits, vegetables and herbs for cooking are grown.

**winter vegetables:** vegetables that can be grown in winter such as carrots, beets, broccoli, winter squash, etc.

**Fruit trees were trained flat against the wall:** There were fruit trees planted next to the wall. As they grew, their branches were attached to the wall (usually with wires) so they grew flat against the wall in a pretty pattern.

**glass frames:** glass boxes placed over plants to warm and protect them in cold weather.

**touched his cap:** touched his cap with his hand as a respectful greeting.

**nowt:** nothing.

**bird with a bright red breast:** English robin. English robins are smaller, rounder and more colorful than American robins and they are known for their curiosity and friendliness.

**tha' cheeky little beggar:** *(British)* thou (you) cheeky (amusing but bold) little beggar (a teasing word meaning a person).

**Has tha' begun tha' courtin' this early in the season?:** Has thou (you) begun thy (your) courting (looking for a mate) this early in the season?

**Tha'rt too forrad:** Thou (You) art (are) too forward (bold).

**there never was his like for curiosity an' meddlin':** there never was his equal (anyone to match him) for being curious and getting involved in others' business.

**hissel:** himself.

**Art tha' th' little wench from India?:** Are thou (you) the little wench (girl) from India?

**We was wove out of th' same cloth:** We were woven out of the same cloth, meaning we are very similar.

**Dang me if he hasn't took a fancy to thee:** Dang me (a mild swear) if he hasn't taken a fancy (liking) to you.

**heather-bells:** bell-shaped flowers on heather plants.

**rose-trees:** rose bushes.

**uncompaniable:** unfriendly.

**None as any one can find, an' none as is any one's business:** None (no door) that anyone can find and none that is anyone's business.

**Don't you be a meddlesome wench an' poke your nose where it's no cause to go:** Don't you be a meddlesome (interfering) wench (girl) and poke your nose where it shouldn't go.

**Get you gone an' play you:** Go away and play.

## Chapter 5

**Tha' got on well enough with that this mornin', didn't tha':** Thou (you) got along well enough (did well) with that this morning, didn't thee (you).

**pattering:** running with quick, light steps.

**darting:** quick and sudden.

**blow the cobwebs out of her young brain:** *(British)* get rid of feelings of tiredness and confusion.

**great servant's hall:** large room where servants ate and gathered when they weren't working. The servant's hall was usually by the kitchen and downstairs from the main house.

**upperhousemaids:** senior housemaids who worked upstairs waiting on members of the family. These maids were usually better educated and spoke more formal English.

**wutherin':** wuthering; blowing strongly with a rushing, roaring sound.

**bare stand up:** barely stand up straight.

**shuddering:** sounding like it is shaking violently and quickly.

**buffeting it:** striking against it repeatedly.

**red coal fire:** slow-burning lumps of coal that produce very little flame but heat a room for a long time.

**store:** *(context: "Then Martha gave up her store of knowledge.")* great quantity or large collection.

**Mind:** keep in mind; remember.

**'tend:** short for attend to (take care of).

## Chapter 6

**moithered:** *(Yorkshire)* bothered; harrassed.

**cow-shed:** *(British)* a rough building where cows are taken to be milked or when the weather is cold or stormy.

**moorland:** an area of the moor (wild countryside covered with grasses, small bushes and usually no trees).

**Tha'st old enough to be learnin' thy book a good bit now:** Thou is (you are) old enough to be learning your book (learning to read and learning things from reading) a good bit (a lot) now.

**housekeeper's sitting-room:** A "sitting room" is a private room where people can sit and talk or read, sew, etc. Mrs. Medlock, as the housekeeper, is senior to all the other servants except Pitcher, the butler, so next to her bedroom, she has her own sitting room.

**below stairs:** *(British)* down stairs from the main house where the kitchen and the servants' rooms are.

**waited on her, hand and foot:** acted as her servant and did everything possible for her.

**Sometimes tha' looks fair soft in th' head:** *(British)* Sometimes thou (you) look fair soft in the head (fairly stupid).

**authority:** somebody in a position of power, as Mrs. Medlock has power over Mary and Martha.

**second floor:** third floor. What Americans call the first floor is called the ground floor in Europe. So, the second floor in America is called the first floor in Europe.

**inlaid furniture:** furniture decorated with patterns of small pieces of wood, ivory, etc., set into the surface.

**leaded panes:** Panes are sheets of glass in a window or door. Leaded panes are smaller panes fixed in place by thin strips of lead making a pattern in a larger window.

**lady's sitting room:** a room next to the lady's bedroom to sit, talk, read, sew, eat, etc., privately. A lady's sitting room would be larger with much finer furniture and decorations than a housekeeper's sitting room.

**mahouts:** men who cared for and drove elephants when transporting people or materials.

**palanquins:** large boxes usually covered with colorful cloth for people to ride in. Most palanquins have two long poles on either side that are carried by four or more people. An elephant's palanquin is placed on its back.

**obliged to:** found it necessary to.

**look sharp after:** pay close attention to, keep track of.

## Chapter 7

**blazing:** very bright and hot. In hot climates like India, the sun shines so strongly that the sky looks white.

**Nowt o' th' soart:** *(Yorkshire)* Nothing of the sort. Today, we would say "not at all."

**reflectively:** thoughtfully.

**How does tha' like thyself?:** How does thou (you) like thyself (yourself)? Today we would say, "How do you like yourself?"

**talking ill of folk:** criticizing or complaining about other people.

**Tha' young vixon, tha':** Thou young vixen, thou. Today we would say "You young vixen (bad tempered female), you."

**brought me to my senses:** got me to understand that I had been behaving in a stupid way.

**week's baking:** It was the custom to do all the week's baking in one day. Enough bread, cakes, pies, etc. were made to last the week.

**high spirits:** "Spirits" means the way someone is feeling. Someone in high spirits is feeling great.

**good humor:** a cheerful and agreeable mood.

**stirrin' down below in th' dark:** stirring (starting to grow after resting) down below in the dark (underground).

**bits o' green spikes:** small green points that are the new plants growing up.

**daffydowndillys:** daffodils; flowering plants with long narrow green leaves and bright yellow flowers with the center part shaped like a trumpet.

**uncurl a leaf this day an' another that:** uncurl a leaf one day and another leaf on another day.

**Tha's no need:** Thou has no need. Today we would say, "You don't have to."

**flirted his tail:** moved his tail with a sudden, playful jerk.

**waistcoat:** A waistcoat is really a man's vest. Here the author is using it to describe the robin's red breast.

**freshly turned up earth:** newly dug up dirt.

## Chapter 8

**Living as it were, all by herself:** Living as if she were all by herself. "As it were" means in a way; as if it were so.

**baffling:** confusing; hard to figure out.

**all out of the way:** completely done.

**doughcake:** small, round sweet cake.

**My word!:** an exclamation of surprise.

**It would set 'em clean off their heads:** make them crazy with delight.

**York:** a small city in north Yorkshire, England. If Misselthwaite Manor were a real place, York would probably be the closest major city to it.

**our Dickon's eyes nearly started out o' his head:** my brother Dickon's eyes nearly popped out of his head; Dickon was really surprised.

**our 'Lizabeth Ellen:** my sister Elizabeth Ellen.

**skippin'-ropes:** skipping ropes; jump ropes.

**tuppence:** two pennies.

**Martha, tha's brought me thy wages like a good lass, an' I've got four places to put every penny, but I'm just goin' to take tuppence out of it to buy that child a skippin'-rope:** Martha, thou has (you have) brought me your wages (pay) like a good girl and I've got four ways to use every single penny but I'm just going to take two pennies out of it to buy that child a jump rope.

**mystified:** confused by something you can't explain.

**for all:** even though.

**common little cottager:** low class girl who lives in a cottage.

**mount up:** increase the number.

**sensiblest:** most sensible; making the most sense.

**so as tha' wrap up warm:** as long as thou (you) wrap up warmly (put on a warm coat, hat, gloves, etc).

**tha' art a queer, old womanish thing:** thou art (you are) an odd person who acts like an old woman.

**If tha'd been our 'Lizabeth Ellen tha'd have given me a kiss:**
If thou had (you had) been my sister Elizabeth Ellen thou would
have (you would have) given me a kiss.

Note: Some editions say "*It* tha'd been our 'Lizabeth Ellen . . . ."
This is probably a typo.

**If tha' was different, p'raps tha'd want to thysel':** If thou was
(you were) different, perhaps thou would (you would) want to
thyself (yourself).

**P'raps tha' art a young 'un, after all, an' p'raps tha's got child's
blood in thy veins instead of sour buttermilk:** Perhaps thou art
(you are) a young one, after all, and perhaps thou has (you have)
got child's blood in thy (your) veins instead of sour buttermilk
(sour, pale liquid left after churning butter from milk).

**Tha' keep on:** Thou (you) keep doing it.

**Tha' shapes well enough at it for a young 'un that's lived with
heathen:** Thou shapes (performs) well enough at it for a young
one who has lived with heathen (people who don't believe in the
God from the Bible).

**tha' doesn't look sharp:** thou doesn't (you don't) pay close
attention.


## Chapter 9

**standard roses:** roses trained so that the leaves and flowers grow
at the top of a straight bare stem.

**hazy:** unclear to look at, as though covered by mist or smoke.

**mantle:** something that covers something else. In this case, the rose branches are covering most everything in the garden.

**air:** special look and way of acting.

**alcoves of evergreen:** an "alcove" is a smaller private area set apart from a larger area, such as in a house or garden. In this case, the "alcoves of evergreen" probably have evergreen bushes planted around them with openings for someone to walk in.

**flower urns:** decorative containers to hold flowers.

**wondered at:** been filled with amazement and admiration of.

**midday dinner:** lunch.

**helps o' rice pudding:** helpings (servings) of rice pudding (sweet pudding made with rice, milk and sugar).

**narcissusis:** narcissus plants that grow from a bulb similar to a small daffodil with yellow or white flowers.

**purple flags:** deep purple flowers with three petals and narrow green leaves.

**new idea taking possession of her:** a new idea came to mind and took over her thoughts.

**brick walk:** a path with bricks laid into the surface to make a smooth, firm walkway.

**park woods:** (British) woods are a large section of land with many trees growing together. These woods belong to Misselthwaite Manor and are located in its park outside its gardens.

**kingdom:** the secret garden which Mary thinks of as her own kingdom that she can create and control.

**turning matters over in her mind:** thinking things over carefully. "Turning over something in your mind" means to think about something carefully. "Matters" means the things being talked or thought about.

**plant nothin' but parsley an' radishes:** In English cooking, parsley and radishes are mostly used to decorate food so they are not very useful vegetables for feeding a family. Martha's mother means that Mary will benefit from planting and growing things even if they aren't very useful.

**shillings:** a unit of British money. There are 20 shillings in a British pound.

**one and three pence:** one shilling and three pence. There are 12 pence in a shilling.

**This comes hoping to find you well as it leaves me at present:** This letter comes to you hoping you are well as I am right now.

**oat cake:** a thin, flat, slightly sweet cookie made from oats.

**restlessly:** showing an inability to stay still or calm because of worry.

## Chapter 10

**fairy-story:** about fairies and other magic; fairy tale.

**in bloom:** having flowers.

**flightiness:** *(British)* changing friends or activities easily. This is said in a disapproving way.

**as full o' pride as an egg's full o' meat:** completely full of pride. (The "meat" of an egg could be considered everything inside the shell because it is all good for eating.)

**jerked out:** said suddenly with some effort.

**Tha's beginnin' to do Misselthwaite credit:** Thou is (You are) beginning to do Misselthwaite (Manor) credit. This means that by gaining weight and looking healthier (less yellow), Mary will bring praise to Misselthwaite Manor.

**Tha' can put up with me a bit:** Thou (You) can tolerate (get along with) me a little.

**Tha' thinks tha'll get over me by doin' that:** Thou (You) thinks thou (you) will win me over (make me like you) by doing that.

**Tha' thinks no one can stand out against thee:** Thou (You) thinks that no one can resist you.

**I'm danged:** a mild swear to show happy surprise.

**Tha' does know how to get at a chap:** Thou (You) does know how to have an effect on someone; in this case, to get the person to like you.

**bachelder:** bachelor; an unmarried man.

**lodge with Martin at th' gate:** live with Martin at the gatehouse by the entrance to the estate of Misselthwaite Manor.

**taters:** potatoes.

**rheumatics:** rheumatism; a common name for physical conditions where the joints and muscles become stiff and painful.

**rough wooden pipe:** crudely made musical instrument probably like a recorder.

**It'd flight them:** It would scare them away.

**white poppy:** small plant with large, delicate white flowers.

**blue larkspur:** tall plant with many small, blue flowers on a tall stalk. Larkspur is the common name for delphinium which Dickon talks about later in the book. Blue larkspur is one type of delphinium that has very deep blue flowers.

**mignonette:** a plant with spiky leaves and lots of fragrant greenish white flowers.

**He's took thee on:** He's become your friend.

**Birds is rare choosers an' a robin can flout a body worse than a man:** Birds only choose special people for friends and a robin can ignore a person worse than a man can.

**he's making up to thee now:** he's making friends with you now.

**Cannot tha' see a chap?:** Can't you see a fellow? (The robin is showing off and asking Mary to pay attention to him.)

**fledge:** grow feathers for flying.

**there'd be naught safe on th' moor:** there would be nothing safe on the moor.

## Chapter 11

**Missel Thrush:** large, brown song bird with a spotted breast that lives in England. Also known as the Mistle Thrush because it likes to eat mistletoe berries.

**delicatest:** most easily hurt or damaged; weakest.

**it's done for:** it's dead.

**They'll grow now like Jack's bean-stalk:** They'll grow now fast and tall. Jack's bean-stalk was a magic bean plant that grew up to the clouds overnight from the English fairy tale entitled *Jack and the Beanstalk*.

**I wasn't brought up nesh enough:** I wasn't brought up in a delicate or pampered way. (*Nesh* in Yorkshire describes someone who gets cold too easily: "It's cold." "No, it's not. You're just *nesh!*")

**white-thorn knobstick:** a stick with a knob at the end that can be used as a weapon. It is made from the white thorn tree, also called the hawthorn tree, which has very hard wood.

**gardener's garden:** a garden that is carefully tended and kept very neat.

**all clipped an' spick an' span:** all cut back and very neat and tidy.

**bit o' prunin' done here an' there, later than ten year ago:** a little pruning done here and there within the last ten years. Pruning is cutting off dead or unnecessary parts of trees and plants so they will grow better in the future.

**Canterbury bells:** a European plant with bell-shaped blue, pink or white flowers hanging in clusters.

**campanulas:** any of a group of flowering plants with bell-shaped flowers. Canterbury bells are one type of campanulas.

**They'll have growed too close an' we'll have to separate 'em:** They will have grown too close and we'll have to separate them. Lilies of the valley form new plants by sending up shoots off their underground rootlike stem. If they are left to grow on their own for many years, more and more new lily of the valley plants will grow in the same area causing the plants to become more and more crowded together. Gardeners can gently separate the plants and replant them farther apart so they will grow better.

**Run on an' get thy victuals:** Run along and get your food (lunch).

**They likes a bit o' fat wonderful:** Birds love a bit of fat.

**poppy-colored cheeks:** bright red cheeks. Many poppy flowers are a bright red color.

**distended:** puffed out.


## Chapter 12

**delightedly:** with delight or great pleasure.

**head gardener:** the person who plans all the planting and manages the gardening staff of a large estate. A large estate like Misselthwaite Manor can include several different types of gardens such as rose gardens, lawns, kitchen gardens, herb gardens, orchards and walkways with borders and shrubs. There can be buildings such as greenhouses and storage sheds plus fountains, streams or ponds to care for. The head gardener would find out what the owners and the cooks wanted the gardens to look like or produce. He would then direct some of his staff to build the walls, fountains and walkways as needed. He would also direct his gardeners to plant and care for all the flowers, trees, fruits, vegetables and herbs needed.

**under-gardeners:** the gardeners who work for the head gardener.

**crabbed:** grouchy; bad-tempered and being disagreeable on purpose.

**made bold to stop him:** took the bold action of stopping him to talk to him. English life in the early 1900s was still divided by the classes. Mr. Archibald Craven was a member of the upper class and Susan Sowerby was in the poor, lower class. Usually members of the lower class did not speak to people of the upper class unless they were spoken to first, so it was bold of Mrs. Sowerby to stop Mr. Craven to say something to him.

**as put him in th' mind to see you:** that gave him the idea that he should see you.

**distracted:** confused; unable to think clearly.

**charge:** a person that someone must take care of.

**as you'd find in a day's walk:** that you could find in this area (a day's walk might have been 15–30 miles).

**dinner service:** (*British*) A dinner service is all the matching plates, cups, bowls and other dishes needed to serve someone dinner. Martha has removed all the dishes Mary used for her dinner.

**meant for a nest with a bird sitting on it:** meant to look like a nest with a bird sitting on it.

## Chapter 13

**carved four-posted bed hung with brocade:** a bed with four, tall wooden posts, carved with designs, standing up from each corner. Between the posts were rods holding curtains of brocade (thick cloth with designs woven into it).

**locks:** bunches of hair.

**agate gray:** An agate is a hard stone that has different shades of color, usually light blue-gray.

**wrapper:** a loose coat worn over night clothes or by someone not fully dressed; this is also called a "dressing gown," a term used in the next chapter.

**talk me over:** talk about me when they think I can't hear.

**ceased to matter:** stopped being important.

**forgetting herself for a moment:** "to forget yourself" means to forget to be careful about what you say or do; in this case, Mary is forgetting herself and saying something that might start to give away her secret about the garden.

**clambered:** climbed across with difficulty.

**complainingly:** in a complaining, resentful way.

**chanting song:** a soft song with notes that sound similar to each other.

**Hindustani:** India has two official languages: English (brought to India from England) and Hindi (a language native to northern India). There are many versions of the Hindi language. Hindustani is one of them.

## Chapter 14

Note: For the remainder of the glossary when "thou" or "thee" is used in an entry, it will not be noted that these words mean "you."

**Rajah:** a prince or king of India.

**Tha' looks as if tha'd somethin' to say:** Thou looks as if thou had something to say. (See note above.)

**He knows us daren't call our souls our own:** He knows we dare not think or act freely (according to what we believe is right).

**It's as if tha'd walked straight into a lion's den:** It's as if thou had walked straight into a lion's den (home). "To walk into a lion's den" is to go into a dangerous place or to face something that requires a lot of courage, knowing it will likely be very dangerous or cause trouble.

**agitated:** anxious, nervous, upset.

**packed back to mother:** fired from her job and sent home.

**went off his head like:** went crazy.

**'sylum:** asylum; an older word for a hospital for mentally ill people.

**nowt:** stupid, rude person.

**"rose cold":** rose fever; an illness like a cold experienced in the spring or early summer. It is usually caused by grass pollen that is airborne when roses are in bloom.

**threw himself into a passion:** had a temper tantrum.

**bobbing a curtsy:** making a small, quick curtsy as a sign of respect by bending down at the knees briefly.

**set her wondering:** started her wondering about something.

**charm:** to cause a person or animal to do what one wants, as if by magic. (See next entry.)

**snake-charmer:** person who appears to control a snake by playing music on a pipe, usually getting it to rise out of a basket slowly and appear to sway or dance.

**chippering:** making small chirping sounds.

**unsympathetically:** in a way that shows no feeling of sorrow for someone.

**make up his mind to it:** decide that he wants to.

**humor:** mood, state of mind. (In this case, the doctor is saying Colin might live if someone put him in the mood or state of mind that living would be good and worth doing.)

**dressing gown:** A loose coat worn over night clothes or by someone not fully dressed. This is also called a "wrapper."

## Chapter 15

**Tha'rt not nigh so yeller and tha'rt not nigh so scrawny. Even tha' hair doesn't slamp down on tha' head so flat:** Thou art not nearly so yellow and thou art not nearly so skinny. Even thy hair doesn't lie down on thy head so flat. *Nigh* is an older word meaning "nearly or near." *Slamp* is a Yorkshire word meaning "to slap down on or lie flat on."

**Tha'rt not half so ugly when it's that way an' there's a bit o' red in tha' cheeks:** Thou art not half so ugly when it's that way (fluffed out) and there's a little red in thy cheeks.

**blinds:** window coverings made from strips of cloth or wood that can be pulled up or down with a string.

**tender little fluting sounds:** high, clear, soft sounds like little flutes.

**herbaceous beds:** areas of a garden planted with flowering plants that live several years.

**glossy-plumaged:** covered with smooth, shiny feathers.

**glowing:** showing excitement.

**tousled:** rumpled and untidy as though just out of bed.

**Captain he run same as if th' hounds had been after him:** Captain ran as if the hounds had been after him (very fast). Fox hunting is a sport in England where foxes are chased and caught. Hound dogs chase the fox by following his scent. Then people riding horses follow the dogs and try to be first to catch the fox.

**leafbuds:** small swellings that will grow to become leaves on the branches of trees and plants.

**mould:** loose, rich soil.

**warmed springtime breathing:** warm smell of earth coming to life in the spring. The author is making the earth seem like a person by saying it is breathing.

**tumbled:** messed up.

**We munnot stir:** We must not stir (move).

**We munnot scarce breathe:** We must not scarcely (barely) breathe.

**us don't flight him:** we don't scare him.

**He'd be out with us for good if he got th' notion us was interferin' now:** He would be upset with us permanently if he got the idea we were interfering now (with his nest building).

**He's settin' up housekeepin':** He is setting up housekeeping (setting up a place to live with his mate and babies).

**He'll be shyer an' readier to take things ill:** He'll be shyer and more likely to take offense at things.

**I warrant:** I'm certain.

**I'm right down glad:** I'm positively glad.

**in fine trouble:** very worried.

**Them as is not wanted scarce ever thrives:** Those (people) that are not wanted scarcely ever thrive (grow healthy, do well).

**No lad could get well as thought them sort o' things:** No boy could get well while he thought about things like that.

**carriage:** wheelchair.

**Wheres'ever tha' puts it:** Wheresoever (wherever) thou put it.

**Get on with thee, lad:** Get going, young man.

**Tha'st got no time to lose:** Thou hast no time to lose.

## Chapter 16

**He was nigh goin' into one o' his tantrums:** He was nearly going into one of his tantrums. "Nigh" is an old word meaning near or almost.

**There's been a nice to do:** There's been a big fuss.

**pitifulness:** describes the sad or sorry state of a person who has suffered and wants sympathy.

**nice agreeable pair:** "agreeable" normally means friendly and easy to get along with. At this moment, they are completely disagreeable (unfriendly and impossible to get along with) so the author is making fun of them by describing them as an "agreeable pair."

**sprung at each other:** attacked each other.

**rough-and-tumble fight:** disorderly, violent fighting with no rules.

**Mary's face looked as pinched as a nutcracker:** A nutcracker is a tool for cracking open the hard shells of nuts. It is often made to look like a wooden soldier whose mouth is opened, the nut is inserted and then the mouth is forced (pinched) closed to crack the nut.

**pleasure began to crowd her anger out of her mind:** Her pleasure overcame the anger she was feeling so she felt happy again. To crowd something out means to not allow anything into a space or to force it out.

**knitting her brows:** drawing her eyebrows together by wrinkling her forehead in a scowl.

## Chapter 17

**twitching of her mouth:** jerky movement of her mouth, perhaps because she is trying not to smile or laugh.

**long-drawn broken breaths:** deep, uneven breaths. (To "draw" a breath means to breathe in. "Broken" means interrupted, not smooth.)

**soft-hearted:** kind and sympathetic.

**beef tea:** (*British*) a nourishing hot drink made by boiling beef and then straining the liquid from the meat.

**get your sleep out:** probably means get your full night's sleep.

**appealingly:** asking for help in a sincere way.

## Chapter 18

**Tha' Munnot Waste No Time:** Thou must not waste any time.

**Tha' did give it him last night for sure:** Thou certainly did give it to him (yell at him with blunt honesty) last night.

**salt won't save him:** nothing will save him. (Salt was used to keep food from going bad so if salt couldn't keep him from going bad, nothing could.)

**hearken at 'em callin' to each other:** listen to them calling to each other.

**mun:** (*Yorkshire*) must.

**An' we munnot lose no time about it:** And we must not lose any time about doing it. Today, we would say "We must do it right away."

**graidely:** *(Yorkshire)* fine, well or nice looking.

**ax:** ask.

**canna':** can not.

**happen a bud or two:** perhaps a flower bud or two.

**nowt as good for ill folk as laughin' is:** nothing as good for ill people as laughing is.

**'ud cure a chap as was makin' ready for typhus fever:** would cure a person even if he was becoming ill with typhus fever (a serious disease that causes fever and red spots on the skin).

**I canna' talk as graidely as Dickon an' Martha can but tha' sees I can shape a bit:** I can not talk as well as Dickon and Martha but thou can see I can speak it a little. *Shape* is a Yorkshire word meaning to perform, in this case, to perform by speaking Yorkshire.

**An' tha' a Yorkshire lad thysel' bred an' born:** And thou a lad born and grown up in Yorkshire thyself.

## Chapter 19

**It's past crediting:** It's unbelievable. "Crediting" means being able to believe. If something is past crediting, it has gone past the point where you are able to believe it.

**chattering:** fast talking about unimportant or fun things, which goes on and on.

**weak:** lacking in strong beliefs or purpose; easily tempted.

**outright:** openly; without holding back or hiding anything.

**bromide:** medicine to make a person sleepy.

**royal signet rings:** a ring that bears a small symbol or initials that can make a stamp on a document to make it official. A royal signet ring would be worn by a king.

**sick nurse:** someone who nurses sick people back to good health.

**volubly:** talkatively; talking easily with a steady flow of words.

**a bit of a preach:** a little scolding.

**jography:** geography lessons.

**enow:** enough.

**hard knocks:** hardships; misfortunes.

**pips:** seeds.

**stifling:** lacking fresh air.

**hiding:** beating.

**clemmin':** hunger.

**Aquilegia:** (British) the scientific name for the family of flowering plants which includes the columbine. Also, another name for columbine.

## Chapter 20

**scuffle:** move in a hurried, sometimes confused way.

**chair-carriage:** wheelchair.

**ivied:** covered with ivy.

**"bedding-out plants":** small flowering plants that can be planted outside in decorative arrangements for a season or two.

**shrubbery walks:** walkways between plantings of tall bushes (shrubbery), usually evergreen shrubs.

**filtered:** passed gradually from person to person.

**stable yards:** the stables where horses are kept and surrounding areas for working with the horses or carriages. When the author writes that rumors filtered into the stable yards, she is referring to rumors being heard and discussed by the servants who work in the stable yards.

**What's to do now?:** What's happening now?

**His Royal Highness:** This is a correct way to refer to the King of England. Mr. Roach is using this phrase jokingly to refer to Colin.

**back staircase:** The smaller staircases in the back of the house were used by the servants. The family and guests of the house used the larger, fancier front staircases.

**there's them as finds their duties made a lot easier to stand up under:** there are people who find their duties easier to perform.

**Buckingham Palace:** the royal palace in London.

**carven:** carved.

**servitor:** servant.

**water-gardens:** gardens built around fountains, streams or pools of water.

**Royal Family:** the close family members of a reigning king or queen.

**Prince Consort:** a prince married to a reigning queen.

**flute:** make high, clear sounds like a flute.

**wild clear scented sweetness:** fresh, clean air with a pleasant scent from the wild plants on the moor.

**th' bees are at it wonderful today:** the bees are busily working at the gorse wonderfully today.

**witched away:** made to disappear as if by witchcraft.

**fountain beds:** flower beds planted around the fountains.

**snow:** pure white like the color of snow.

**pipes:** musical sounds like those made by recorders or similar pipes. Here it describes birds singing.

## Chapter 21

**tender:** young or new.

**flushing:** glowing with a rosy color.

**East:** place where the sun rises.

**seed one as graidely as this 'ere:** seen one as beautiful as this here (this one).

**Does tha' think as happen it was made loike this 'ere all o' purpose for me?:** Does thou think that it happened to be made like this on purpose for me?

**Tha'rt shapin' first-rate—that tha' art:** Thou art shaping (speaking) first-rate—that thou art. (*Shape* is a Yorkshire word meaning to perform, in this case, to perform by speaking Yorkshire.)

**in state:** in a very formal or grand manner.

**Tha'll see him often enow after a bit:** Thou will see him often enough after a short time.

**When th' eggs hatches out th' little chap he'll be kep' so busy it'll make his head swim:** When the eggs hatch, the little fellow will be kept so busy it will make his head swim (make him dizzy with confusion).

**Tha'll see him flyin' backward an' for'ard carryin' worms nigh as big as himsel' an' that much noise goin' on in th' nest when he gets there as fair flusters him so as he scarce knows which big mouth to drop th' first piece in:** Thou will see him flying back and forth carrying worms nearly as big as himself and so much noise going on in the nest when he gets there that it flusters him so much he scarcely knows which big mouth to drop the first piece in.

**tea:** (*British*) a small meal eaten with tea in the late afternoon.

**rhododendron walk:** a walkway lined with rhododendron bushes. Rhododendrons are evergreen bushes with dark green oval leaves and big clusters of pink, purple or white flowers.

**mellow:** relaxing; easygoing.

**lances:** spears of sunlight.

**That tha' will. Us'll have thee walkin' about here an' diggin' same as other folk afore long:** That thou will. We'll have thee walking about and digging the same as other people before long.

**When tha' stops bein' afraid tha'lt stand on 'em. An' tha'lt stop bein' afraid in a bit:** When thou stops being afraid thou wilt stand on them. And thou wilt stop being afraid in a short time.

**dropped the gray film drowsily over his eyes:** Birds have an additional, thin eyelid that looks like a gray or brown film when closed over the eye. This eyelid is usually closed to clean the eye when resting.

**If I wasn't a bachelder, an' tha' was a wench o' mine, I'd give thee a hidin':** If I weren't a bachelor and thou were a girl (daughter) of mine, I'd give thee a beating.

**I never thowt much o' thee:** I never thought much of thee.

**I couldna' abide thee:** I couldn't abide (stand) thee.

**A scrawny buttermilk-faced young besom, allus askin' questions an' pokin' tha' nose where it wasna' wanted:** A scrawny buttermilk-faced young besom (bad girl or woman), always asking questions and poking thy nose where it wasn't wanted.

**I never knowed how tha' got so thick wi' me:** I'll never know how thou got so thick (friendly, close) with me.

**Tha' young bad 'un:** Thou young bad one.

**Laying tha' badness on a robin—not but what he's impidint enow for anything:** Blaming thy badness on a robin—even though he's impudent enough for anything.

**tha' young nowt:** thou young good-for-nothing.

**State Coach:** royal carriage.

**Tha'rt as thin as a lath an' as white as a wraith, but there's not a knob on thee:** Thou art as thin as a lath (thin, narrow strip of wood) and as white as a wraith (ghost), but there's not a knob (bump) on thee.

**Tha'lt make a mon yet:** Thou wilt become a man yet.

**touched his hat gardener fashion:** probably means touched the front brim of his hat with his thumb and first two fingers. (At the time of this story, servants were expected to show respect to upper class people. As a sign of respect, male servants would remove their hats and female servants would curtsy. These actions were performed so often that they were often shortened so that the men just touched their hat brims without removing them and the women made quick partial curtsies [bobbing curtsies], not full curtsies.)

## Chapter 22

**rug:** (*British*) thick, woolen blanket.

**What art sayin'?:** What are you saying?

**testily:** crossly; irritably.

**Not tha':** Not thou.

**Nowt o' th' sort:** Nothing of the sort. Today, we would say "not at all." Different spelling but same meaning as "Nowt o' th' soart" defined in Chapter 7.

**Th' world's full o' jackasses brayin' an' they never bray nowt but lies:** The world's full of jackasses braying and they never bray nothing but lies. Here jackass means a fool and braying means talking foolishly. This is a way of saying that the world is full of stupid people who like to spread false rumors about other people.

**main:** *(context: "She were* main *fond of it.")* very; extremely.

**Tha' come an' did a bit o' prunin'! I couldn't make out how it had been done:** Thou came and did a little pruning! I couldn't figure out how it had been done.

**Th' rheumatics held me back:** The rheumatism held me back (kept me from doing something).

**nigh:** *(an older word)* near to a place.

**wick:** alive.

**I thowt tha' was just leein' to please me:** I thought thou was just lying to please me.

**that sounds as if tha'd got wits enow:** that sounds as if thou had got wits (intelligence) enough.

**broke the pot from the mould:** *(British)* Mould is soft, rich soil good for growing plants. At this time, plants were potted in red clay pots that broke easily. To plant a potted flowering plant, the flower pot was often broken away from the mould around the roots of the plant before the plant was placed in the ground.

## Chapter 23

**brute:** thoughtless person; someone unaware and uncaring about the feelings of others.

**undisturbedly:** calmly; showing he was not bothered.

**black:** (*context: "It's Magic, but not black."*) referring to black magic—magic attempted for evil purposes, calling upon evil spirits or the devil.

**It's as white as snow:** referring to white magic—magic practiced for good purposes or to stop black magic or evil.

**She liked them things as was allus pointin' up to th' blue sky:** She liked those things that were always pointing up to the blue sky.

**Not as she was one o' them as looked down on th' earth:** Not that she was one of them that looked down on the earth. "To look down on" here means to think of something or someone as less important, not as good or worthless.

**fakirs:** traveling religious men who live by begging and can perform amazing acts such as walking on hot coals or sleeping on nails without hurting themselves.

**Summat allus come o' that:** Something always came of (happened because of) that.

**He gave her a good hidin' an' went to th' Blue Lion an' got as drunk as a lord:** He gave her a good beating and went to the Blue

Lion (a pub or bar) and got as drunk as a lord (very drunk from alcohol).

**She'd be rare an' pleased if th' sinetifik 'speriment worked—an' so 'ud Jem:** She'd be unusually pleased if the scientific experiment worked—and so would Jem.

**devotees:** dedicated members of a religious group.

**prayer-meeting:** gathering to pray to God, usually less formal than a Sunday morning service.

**agen:** *(Yorkshire)* against.

**dervishes:** members of certain Muslim religious groups that have energetic dances or movements as part of their religious practices.

**The sermon was good enow—but I'm bound to get out afore th' collection:** The sermon (religious speech) was good enough— but I'm determined to leave before the collection. In Christian churches, the collection is donation money that is collected from people in church after the sermon is completed.

**Tha'lt end wi' winnin' th' Belt an' bein' champion prize-fighter of all England:** Thou wilt end with winning the Belt (championship belt awarded to the best prizefighter) and being champion prizefighter of all England.

**Ax pardon:** Ask pardon, meaning "I ask your pardon."

## Chapter 24

**get on as comfortable:** get on as comfortably. "Get on" means to have enough food or money to live.

**flavor with 'em as nobody's has:** flavor that nobody else's potatoes have.

**It's been th' makin' o' her an' th' savin' o' him:** It's been the making of her and the saving of him. "Been the making of her" means caused her to develop good characteristics.

**plump up:** gain weight; fatten up.

**cottage loaf:** (British) a large, round loaf of bread with a smaller round piece on top.

**take off th' edge o' their hunger:** take off the edge of their hunger, which means to make the hunger less strong by eating a little bit of food.

**'ud polish off th' corners:** would polish off the corners. "Polish off" means to finish something quickly and completely, in this case, completely finish or satisfy their hunger. Here, "corners" means the outside edges or the rest of their hunger.

**pother:** fuss; worry and conversation about something.

**clotted cream:** (British) lumps of thick cream made by heating fresh milk and skimming the cream off when it comes the top.

**draughts:** (British) swallows.

**stimulating:** encouraging new ideas.

**hammer:** a heavy metal ball attached to a handle by a flexible wire. Hammer throwing is a sport where the person who throws the hammer the farthest wins.

## Chapter 25

**fledged:** had grown wing feathers and were able to fly.

**setting:** sitting on eggs to hatch them.

**outbreak:** outburst; sudden show of emotion or energy.

## Chapter 26

**aught:** *(British—an older word)* whatever; anything.

**held forth:** lectured at great length.

**devouring:** watching or taking in greedily with the eyes.

**tha' calves an' tha' shoulders:** thy calves and thy shoulders.

**pair o' scales:** scales are a device for weighing something. It was probably called a pair of scales because there were two trays or shallow bowls balanced at a central point. You place the thing you want to weigh in one tray and add certain weights to the other tray until they balance.

**rapturous:** full of joy or delight.

**Doxology:** a song of praise to God sung in Christian church services.

**skylards:** This is an error. It should say "skylarks."

**Heavenly Host:** A host is a great number of people or things. The Heavenly Host means the angels of Heaven.

**Father, Son and Holy Ghost:** In Christian belief, the Father is God and the Son is Jesus Christ. The Holy Ghost means different things to different Christians. It is usually thought of as the spirit or love of God. In fact, when most Christians speak of "God," they think of all three of these together.

**raspingly:** with a harsh, scratchy sound.

**tha'rt so like thy mother tha' made my heart jump:** thou art so like your mother thou made my heart jump. To make someone's heart jump is to cause a sudden emotional reaction of some sort.

**drumsticks i' stockin':** drumsticks in stockings. Drumsticks are the lower parts of a bird's leg which are very thin.

**bandy an' knock-kneed:** "Bandy" means having legs that curve outward; bowlegged. "Knock-kneed" means having knees turned inward so they are close together.

**blush rose:** a light pink rose. This is used to describe someone with delicate, soft beauty.

**fou:** foul.

**worrit:** *(Yorkshire)* worry.

**Tha' wert singin':** Thou wert singing.

**what's names to th' Joy Maker:** of what importance are names to God.

## Chapter 27

**Austrian Tyrol:** (*also spelled "Tirol"*) region in western Austria in the Alps.

**face:** (*context: "Mr. Craven looked over...he awoke to the* face *that they were a healthy likable lot."*) Showing up in some editions of the book, this word is an error. It should say "...he awoke to the fact that they..."

**golden sovereign:** a gold coin that had the value of one British pound, probably equivalent to about $125.00 today. Martha's and Dickon's father earned 16 shillings per week and 20 shillings made one sovereign (one pound).

**half a crown:** one eighth of a sovereign or 2½ shillings, probably equivalent to about $15.00 today.

**embowered:** covered or surrounded in a private, quiet place by leafy and flowering vines or branches.

**sup up:** (*Northern British*) drink up by sips.

**I didna' hear that along o' only bein' on the step-ladder lookin' over th' wall:** I didn't hear that because I was only on the stepladder looking over the wall.

# APPENDIX

# ALPHABETICAL WORD LIST

| Word | Chapter |
| --- | --- |
| agate gray | 13 |
| agen | 23 |
| agitated | 14 |
| air | 9 |
| alcoves of evergreen | 9 |
| all clipped an' spick an' span | 11 |
| all out of the way | 8 |
| an' | 4 |
| An' tha' a Yorkshire lad thysel' bred an' born | 18 |
| An' tha's browt th' young 'un with thee | 3 |
| An' we munnot lose no time about it | 18 |
| appealingly | 17 |
| Aquilegia | 19 |
| Art tha' th' little wench from India? | 4 |
| as full o' pride as an egg's full o' meat | 10 |
| as put him in th' mind to see you | 12 |
| as you'd find in a day's walk | 12 |
| at all events | 3 |
| attracted | 2 |
| aught | 26 |
| Austrian Tyrol | 27 |
| authority | 6 |
| avenue | 3 |
| ax | 18 |
| Ax pardon | 23 |
| Ayah | 1 |
| bachelder | 10 |
| back staircase | 20 |

| Word | Chapter |
|------|---------|
| baffling | 8 |
| bandy an' knock-kneed | 26 |
| bare stand up | 5 |
| "bedding-out plants" | 20 |
| beef tea | 17 |
| below stairs | 6 |
| bird with a bright red breast | 4 |
| Birds is rare choosers an' a robin can flout a body worse than a man | 10 |
| bit of a preach (a) | 19 |
| bit o' prunin' done here an' there, later than ten year ago | 11 |
| bits o' green spikes | 7 |
| black | 23 |
| black crepe hat | 2 |
| blackingbrush | 4 |
| blacks | 4 |
| black's a man an' a brother (a) | 4 |
| blazing | 7 |
| blinds | 15 |
| blow the cobwebs out of her young brain | 5 |
| blue larkspur | 10 |
| blush rose | 26 |
| bobbing a curtsy | 14 |
| brick walk | 9 |
| broke the pot from the mould | 22 |
| bromide | 19 |
| brougham | 3 |
| brought me to my senses | 7 |
| brute | 23 |
| Buckingham Palace | 20 |
| buffeting it | 5 |

| Word | Chapter |
|---|---|
| button boots | 4 |
| campanulas | 11 |
| canna' | 18 |
| Canna' tha' dress thysen! | 4 |
| Cannot tha' see a chap? | 10 |
| Canterbury bells | 11 |
| Captain he run same as if th' hounds had been after him | 15 |
| carriage | 15 |
| carved four-posted bed hung with brocade | 13 |
| carven | 20 |
| ceased to matter | 13 |
| chair-carriage | 20 |
| chanting song | 13 |
| charge | 12 |
| charm | 14 |
| chattering | 19 |
| chippering | 14 |
| clambered | 13 |
| clemmin' | 19 |
| clipped borders | 4 |
| clotted cream | 24 |
| common fine bonnet | 2 |
| common little cottager | 8 |
| common, highly colored face | 2 |
| complainingly | 13 |
| compound | 1 |
| cottage loaf | 24 |
| cow-shed | 6 |
| crabbed | 12 |
| daffydowndillys | 7 |
| Dang me if he hasn't took a fancy to thee | 4 |

| Word | Chapter |
| --- | --- |
| darting | 5 |
| day out | 4 |
| delicatest | 11 |
| delightedly | 12 |
| dervishes | 23 |
| devotees | 23 |
| devouring | 26 |
| dinner service | 12 |
| distended | 11 |
| distracted | 12 |
| Does tha' think as happen it was made loike this 'ere all o' purpose for me? | 21 |
| Don't you be a meddlesome wench an' poke your nose where it's no cause to go | 4 |
| doughcake | 8 |
| Doxology | 26 |
| draughts | 24 |
| dressing gown | 14 |
| dropped the gray film drowsily over his eyes | 21 |
| drumsticks i' stockin' | 26 |
| dying like flies | 1 |
| East | 21 |
| embowered | 27 |
| English Government | 1 |
| enow | 19 |
| face | 27 |
| fairy-story | 10 |
| fakirs | 23 |
| familiarly | 1 |
| fatal form | 1 |
| Father, Son and Holy Ghost | 26 |
| filtered | 20 |

| Word | Chapter |
|------|---------|
| flavor with 'em as nobody's has | 24 |
| fledge | 10 |
| fledged | 25 |
| flight of steps | 3 |
| flightiness | 10 |
| flirted his tail | 7 |
| flower urns | 9 |
| flushing | 21 |
| flute | 20 |
| footman | 3 |
| for all | 8 |
| forgetting herself for a moment | 13 |
| fou | 26 |
| fountain beds | 20 |
| freshly turned up earth | 7 |
| fretful | 1 |
| Fruit trees were trained flat against the wall | 4 |
| garden | 1 |
| gardener's garden | 11 |
| gardens | 2 |
| gave me the place | 4 |
| get on as comfortable | 24 |
| Get on with thee, lad | 15 |
| Get you gone an' play you | 4 |
| get your sleep out | 17 |
| glass frames | 4 |
| glossy-plumaged | 15 |
| glowing | 15 |
| golden sovereign | 27 |
| good humor | 7 |
| gorse | 3 |
| graidely | 18 |

| Word | Chapter |
|------|---------|
| great servant's hall | 5 |
| half a crown | 27 |
| hall | 3 |
| hammer | 24 |
| happen a bud or two | 18 |
| hard knocks | 19 |
| Has tha' begun tha' courtin' this early in the season? | 4 |
| hazy | 9 |
| He gave her a good hidin' an' went to th' Blue Lion an' got as drunk as a lord | 23 |
| He knows us daren't call our souls our own | 14 |
| He was nigh goin' into one o' his tantrums | 16 |
| He'd be out with us for good if he got th' notion us was interferin' now | 15 |
| He'll be shyer an' readier to take things ill | 15 |
| he's making up to thee now | 10 |
| He's settin' up housekeepin' | 15 |
| He's took thee on | 10 |
| head gardener | 12 |
| hearken at 'em callin' to each other | 18 |
| hearth-rug | 4 |
| heather-bells | 4 |
| Heavenly Host | 26 |
| held forth | 26 |
| helps o' rice pudding | 9 |
| herbaceous beds | 15 |
| hiding | 19 |
| high spirits | 7 |
| highroad | 3 |
| Hindustani | 13 |
| His Royal Highness | 20 |

| Word | Chapter |
|---|---|
| hissel | 4 |
| housekeeper's sitting-room | 6 |
| How does tha' like thyself? | 7 |
| How's thy Missus? | 3 |
| humor | 14 |
| I canna' talk as graidely as Dickon an' Martha can but tha' sees I can shape a bit | 18 |
| I couldna' abide thee | 21 |
| I didna' hear that along o' only bein' on the step-ladder lookin' over th' wall | 27 |
| I never knowed how tha' got so thick wi' me | 21 |
| I never thowt much o' thee | 21 |
| I thowt tha' was just leein' to please me | 22 |
| I warrant | 15 |
| I wasn't brought up nesh enough | 11 |
| If I wasn't a bachelder, an' tha' was a wench o' mine, I'd give thee a hidin' | 21 |
| If tha' was different, p'raps tha'd want to thysel' | 8 |
| If tha'd been our 'Lizabeth Ellen tha'd have given me a kiss | 8 |
| I'm danged | 10 |
| I'm right down glad | 15 |
| imploringly | 1 |
| impudent blue eyes | 2 |
| in bloom | 10 |
| in fine trouble | 15 |
| in state | 21 |
| inlaid furniture | 6 |
| it had broken out | 1 |
| It would set 'em clean off their heads | 8 |
| It'd flight them | 10 |

| Word | Chapter |
|---|---|
| It's as if tha'd walked straight into a lion's den | 14 |
| It's as white as snow | 23 |
| It's been th' makin' o' her an' th' savin' o' him | 24 |
| It's covered wi' growin' things as smells sweet | 4 |
| it's done for | |
| It's fair lovely in spring an' summer when th' gorse an' broom an' heather's in flower | 4 |
| It's none bare | 4 |
| It's past crediting | 19 |
| ivied | 20 |
| jerked out | 10 |
| jography | 19 |
| kingdom | 9 |
| kitchen-gardens | 4 |
| knitting her brows | 16 |
| lady's sitting room | 6 |
| lances | 21 |
| Laying tha' badness on a robin—not but what he's impidint enow for anything | 21 |
| leaded panes | 6 |
| leafbuds | 15 |
| learn her letters | 1 |
| let upstairs | 4 |
| Living as it were, all by herself | 8 |
| locks | 13 |
| lodge | 3 |
| lodge with Martin at th' gate | 10 |
| long-drawn broken breaths | 17 |
| look sharp after | 6 |
| lowbuilt | 3 |

| Word | Chapter |
|---|---|
| lunchbasket | 3 |
| made bold to stop him | 12 |
| mahouts | 6 |
| main | 22 |
| make up his mind to it | 14 |
| mantle | 9 |
| mantle with jet fringe | 2 |
| Martha, tha's brought me thy wages like a good lass, an' I've got four places to put every penny, but I'm just goin' to take tuppence out of it to buy that child a skippin'-rope | 8 |
| Mary's face looked as pinched as a nutcracker | 16 |
| meant for a nest with a bird sitting on it | 12 |
| mellow | 21 |
| Mem Sahib | 1 |
| Mercy on us | 1 |
| midday dinner | 9 |
| mignonette | 10 |
| Mind | 5 |
| Missel Thrush | 11 |
| Missie Sahib | 1 |
| Mistress Mary Quite Contrary | 2 |
| moithered | 6 |
| moorland | 6 |
| mould | 15 |
| mount up | 8 |
| mounted the box | 3 |
| mun | 18 |
| my mother's put to it | 4 |
| My word! | 8 |
| mystified | 8 |

| Word | Chapter |
|---|---|
| narcissusis | 9 |
| new idea taking possession of her | 9 |
| nice agreeable pair | 16 |
| nigh | 22 |
| No lad could get well as thought them sort o' things | 15 |
| None as any one can find, an' none as is any one's business | 4 |
| Not as she was one o' them as looked down on th' earth | 23 |
| Not but that | 2 |
| Not tha' | 22 |
| nowt (nothing) | 4 |
| nowt (stupid, rude person) | 14 |
| nowt as good for ill folk as laughin' is | 18 |
| Nowt o' th' soart | 7 |
| Nowt o' th' sort | 22 |
| o' | 4 |
| oat cake | 9 |
| obliged to | 6 |
| one and three pence | 9 |
| Our Dickon | 4 |
| our Dickon's eyes nearly started out o' his head | 8 |
| our 'Lizabeth Ellen | 8 |
| outbreak | 25 |
| outright | 19 |
| packed back to mother | 14 |
| pair o' scales | 26 |
| palanquins | 6 |
| park | 2 |
| park gates | 3 |

| Word | Chapter |
|------|---------|
| park woods | 9 |
| passion | 1 |
| pattering | 5 |
| pettish | 2 |
| pig | 1 |
| pipes | 20 |
| pips | 19 |
| Pitcher | 2 |
| pitifulness | 16 |
| plain enough | 4 |
| plain little piece of goods | 2 |
| plant nothin' but parsley an' radishes | 9 |
| playing | 4 |
| pleasure began to crowd her anger out of her mind | 16 |
| plump up | 24 |
| poppy-colored cheeks | 11 |
| pother | 24 |
| P'raps tha' art a young 'un, after all, an' p'raps tha's got child's blood in thy veins instead of sour buttermilk | 8 |
| prayer-meeting | 23 |
| Prince Consort | 20 |
| pronouncing his words in a queer broad fashion | 3 |
| public house | 3 |
| purple flags | 9 |
| railway carriage | 2 |
| Rajah | 14 |
| ramble | 3 |
| rapturous | 26 |
| raspingly | 26 |

| Word | Chapter |
|---|---|
| red coal fire | 5 |
| reflectively | 7 |
| restlessly | 9 |
| rheumatics | 10 |
| rhododendron walk | 21 |
| Riquet a la Houppe | 2 |
| rockery | 2 |
| "rose cold" | 14 |
| rose-trees | 4 |
| rough | 3 |
| rough wooden pipe | 10 |
| rough-and-tumble fight | 16 |
| Royal Family | 20 |
| royal signet rings | 19 |
| rug | 22 |
| Run on an' get thy victuals | 11 |
| Saidie | 1 |
| salaams | 4 |
| salt won't save him | 18 |
| scarce | 4 |
| scrawny buttermilk-faced young besom, allus askin' questions an' pokin' tha' nose where it wasna' wanted (A) | 21 |
| scuffle | 20 |
| scullery-maid | 4 |
| second floor | 6 |
| seed one as graidely as this 'ere | 21 |
| self-absorbed | 2 |
| sensiblest | 8 |
| sermon was good enow—but I'm bound to get out afore th' collection (The) | 23 |
| servants' quarters | 1 |

| Word | Chapter |
| --- | --- |
| servitor | 20 |
| set her wondering | 14 |
| setting | 25 |
| She liked them things as was allus pointin' up to th' blue sky | 23 |
| She'd be rare an' pleased if th' sinetifik 'speriment worked—an' so 'ud Jem | 23 |
| shillings | 9 |
| shrubbery walks | 20 |
| shuddering | 5 |
| sick nurse | 19 |
| sixteen shilling | 4 |
| skin was yellow | 1 |
| skippin'-ropes | 8 |
| skylards | 26 |
| snake-charmer | 14 |
| snow | 20 |
| so as tha' wrap up warm | 8 |
| soft-hearted | 17 |
| Sometimes tha' looks fair soft in th' head | 6 |
| sprung at each other | 16 |
| stable yards | 20 |
| "stand no nonsense from young ones" | 2 |
| standard roses | 9 |
| State Coach | 21 |
| station-master | 3 |
| stifling | 19 |
| stimulating | 24 |
| stirrin' down below in th' dark | 7 |
| stone court | 3 |
| store | 5 |
| strong | 1 |

| Word | Chapter |
|---|---|
| Summat allus come o' that | 23 |
| sup up | 27 |
| 'sylum | 14 |
| take off th' edge o' their hunger | 24 |
| talk me over | 13 |
| talking ill of folk | 7 |
| taters | 10 |
| tea | 21 |
| ten to one | 2 |
| 'tend | 5 |
| tender | 21 |
| tender little fluting sounds | 15 |
| testily | 22 |
| th' | 4 |
| th' bees are at it wonderful today | 20 |
| Th' rheumatics held me back | 22 |
| Th' world's full o' jackasses brayin' an' they never bray nowt but lies | 22 |
| tha | 4 |
| tha' art a queer, old womanish thing | 8 |
| tha' calves an' tha' shoulders | 26 |
| Tha' can put up with me a bit | 10 |
| tha' cheeky little beggar | 4 |
| Tha' come an' did a bit o' prunin'! I couldn't make out how it had been done | 22 |
| Tha' did give it him last night for sure | 18 |
| Tha' does know how to get at a chap | 10 |
| tha' doesn't look sharp | 8 |
| Tha' got on well enough with that this mornin', didn't tha' | 5 |
| Tha' keep on | 8 |
| Tha' looks as if tha'd somethin' to say | 14 |

| Word | Chapter |
|---|---|
| Tha' Munnot Waste No Time | 18 |
| Tha' shapes well enough at it for a young 'un that's lived with heathen | 8 |
| Tha' thinks no one can stand out against thee | 10 |
| Tha' thinks tha'll get over me by doin' that | 10 |
| Tha' wert singin' | 26 |
| Tha' young bad 'un | 21 |
| tha' young nowt | 21 |
| Tha' young vixon, tha' | 7 |
| tha'll | 4 |
| Tha'll see him flyin' backward an' for'ard carryin' worms nigh as big as himsel' an' that much noise goin' on in th' nest when he gets there as fair flusters him so as he scarce knows which big mouth to drop th' first piece in | 21 |
| Tha'll see him often enow after a bit | 21 |
| tha'lt | 4 |
| Tha'lt end wi' winnin' th' Belt an' bein' champion prize-fighter of all England | 23 |
| Tha'lt make a mon yet | 21 |
| tha'rt | 4 |
| Tha'rt as thin as a lath an' as white as a wraith, but there's not a knob on thee | 21 |
| Tha'rt not half so ugly when it's that way an' there's a bit o' red in tha' cheeks | 15 |
| Tha'rt not nigh so yeller and tha'rt not nigh so scrawny. Even tha' hair doesn't slamp down on tha' head so flat | 15 |
| Tha'rt shapin' first-rate—that tha' art | 21 |

| Word | Chapter |
|---|---|
| tha'rt so like thy mother tha' made my heart jump | 26 |
| Tha'rt too forrad | 4 |
| tha's | 3 |
| Tha's beginnin' to do Misselthwaite credit | 10 |
| Tha's no need | 7 |
| Tha'st got no time to lose | 15 |
| Tha'st old enough to be learnin' thy book a good bit now | 6 |
| that sounds as if tha'd got wits enow | 22 |
| That tha' will. Us'll have thee walkin' about here an' diggin' same as other folk afore long | 21 |
| Them as is not wanted scarce ever thrives | 15 |
| there never was his like for curiosity an' meddlin' | 4 |
| there'd be naught safe on th' moor | 10 |
| There's been a nice to do | 16 |
| there's them as finds their duties made a lot easier to stand up under | 20 |
| They likes a bit o' fat wonderful | 11 |
| They'll grow now like Jack's bean-stalk | 11 |
| They'll have growed too close an' we'll have to separate 'em | 11 |
| This comes hoping to find you well as it leaves me at present | 9 |
| threw himself into a passion | 14 |
| toddling thing | 1 |
| touched his cap | 4 |
| touched his hat gardener fashion | 21 |
| tousled | 15 |
| trifle (a) | 2 |

| Word | Chapter |
|---|---|
| trunk | 2 |
| tumbled | 15 |
| tuppence | 8 |
| turning matters over in her mind | 9 |
| twitching of her mouth | 17 |
| 'ud cure a chap as was makin' ready for typhus fever | 18 |
| 'ud polish off th' corners | 24 |
| uncompaniable | 4 |
| uncurl a leaf this day an' another that | 7 |
| under housemaids | 4 |
| under-gardeners | 12 |
| undisturbedly | 23 |
| unresponsive | 2 |
| unsympathetically | 14 |
| upperhousemaids | 5 |
| us don't flight him | 15 |
| volubly | 19 |
| waistcoat | 7 |
| waited on her, hand and foot | 6 |
| warmed springtime breathing | 15 |
| water-gardens | 20 |
| waterproofs | 3 |
| We munnot scarce breathe | 15 |
| We munnot stir | 15 |
| We was wove out of th' same cloth | 4 |
| weak | 19 |
| week's baking | 7 |
| Well enow | 3 |
| went off his head like | 14 |
| West Wing | 2 |
| What art sayin'? | 22 |

| Word | Chapter |
|---|---|
| what's names to th' Joy Maker | 26 |
| What's to do now? | 20 |
| When th' eggs hatches out th' little chap he'll be kep' so busy it'll make his head swim | 21 |
| When tha' stops bein' afraid tha'lt stand on 'em. An' tha'lt stop bein' afraid in a bit | 21 |
| Wheres'ever tha' puts it | 15 |
| white poppy | 10 |
| white-thorn knobstick | 11 |
| wick | 22 |
| wild clear scented sweetness | 20 |
| winter vegetables | 4 |
| witched away | 20 |
| without seeming the least out of temper | 4 |
| wondered at | 9 |
| worrit | 26 |
| wrapper | 13 |
| wutherin' | 5 |
| York | 8 |
| Yorkshire | 2 |
| You ought to have gone to the hills two weeks ago | 1 |

# REFERENCES

*Encarta Dictionary*, North American Edition.

*Random House Unabridged Dictionary*, 1971.

*Webster's New World Student's Dictionary*, 1996.

*Cambridge International Dictionary of English*, 2002.

*Oxford Compact English Dictionary*, 2004.

*Dictionary of Family Names*, Oxford University Press.

*American Heritage Dictionary of the English Language*, 2003.

*Webster's New International Dictionary of the English Language*, 1924.

*Longman's Advanced American Dictionary*, 2005.

*The Annotated Secret Garden*, edited by Gretchen Holbrook Gerzina, 2007.

*The Secret Garden*, Norton Critical edition, 2006.

## ONLINE SOURCES

Onelook.com

Dictionary.com

Bartleby.com

Merriam Webster's online dictionary

www.cdc.gov

www.greatbritishgardens.co.uk

www.botanical.com

http://home-and-garden.webshots.com

www.glossary.gardenweb.com

www.independent.co.uk

http://www.garden-birds.co.uk/birds/mistlethrush

www.uk-birds.org.uk

www.ups.edu/x6263.xml (Avian anatomy glossary)

www.moneycentral.msn.com

www.goldsovereigns.co.uk

www.businessballs.com

www.1860-1960.com/shoes

www.bardweb.net

www.pitt.edu

www.gardening.wsu.edu

www.anbq.gov.au

www.bbc.co.uk/northyorkshire/voices2005/glossary/glossary.shtml

www.phrases.org.uk

www.peevish.co.uk

http://www.yorkshire-dialect.org/dictionary.htm

www.learnenglishfeelgood.com

www.greydragon.org

9 780897 390880